# An
# Abundance
# of Rain

# Poems and Stories

Bill Worden

Other books by Bill Worden:

*A Kansas Love Story*

# Table of Contents

# Forward

You're probably wondering where I came up with the title for this book, Well, actually my friend, Jody Zilske, used the title of one of my own poems, and I thought it perfect since "An Abundance of Rain" pretty much described how I felt immediately following my wife's death. At this point in my life, the lyrics of a famous Willie Nelson authored song resonated even more clearly—"Funny How Time Slips Away."

My first book, *A Kansas Love Story*, was an autobiography and basically told of my life growing up in several places around the Eastern part of the country, mostly Upstate New York. The book, however, centered around how I met my wife, Janna, who sadly passed away on Christmas day 2021.

During the latter of our nearly sixty years together for reasons I don't know, I suddenly took an interest in writing poems. Writing came naturally to me since it was my profession. I was a journalist and television news anchor for most of my professional life, but poems? Why poems?

I don't have an answer to that other than to say I began being inspired by words that would come to me or phrases I found filled with emotion, pathos, humor or joy.

Words are powerful things, especially when used to portray situations that change peoples' lives or give them pause to stop and think about something. Words can cut deeper than a dagger and leave pain behind even long after the "knife" is removed. Words can also convey happiness, pride, and joy of life.

So, sometime in the decade of the eighties I began writing poems. I had no direction, other than an idea or a thought, perhaps an inspiration. This book contains all twenty poems that I wrote over a period of some twenty-plus years. I would write them and then share them with Janna, then file them away.

As I continued writing them, the subject matter became more interesting to her. Some of them were about her, some about me and some about nothing in particular, save an effort to elicit a laugh or two from the reader.

Some of the poems have a "surprise" ending so, fair warning—if you want to get full enjoyment out of these, don't cheat and skip ahead to the ending. Each chapter is a self-contained story. There are twenty poems, therefore twenty chapters.

This is the kind of book you can pick up and read in bits at a time if you wish, but each poem should provide some insight into your own life through our experiences.

This book is really a promise kept because as I proceeded to continue writing poems, Janna said, "I think you should publish these. These are really good and I think others would enjoy them."

My feeling was always that I didn't just want to write a book of poems, but because I still had no direction to go with the project, it sat on the shelf and on my computer for a few years.

Janna was always looking out for me. In fact, shortly before she passed away, she insisted that I buy a particular expensive laptop that I had wanted, even to the point of constantly asking me, only days before she passed, if I had "ordered that laptop yet."

I was busy caring for her and hadn't thought about it nor ordered it, but she kept insisting. "I want you to order it, please," she said, emphatically. So I finally did.

The poems are not organized chronologically, but rather topically to sort of fit the lives we led, and again there are some humorous breaks along the way and some spiritual insights in this book as well.

And so now I am keeping that other promise she wanted—to publish my poems. She loved them and felt I should share them with others. They are a potpourri if you will.

If you read my first book, the first poem will resonate with you because it's about her and our earliest days together, how we met and so on.

I think you'll enjoy it all. At least I hope you will.

# Chapter 1

*Walks with the Girl I Love*

When Janna and I were first dating, she lived in a modest ranch with her family in a middle-income neighborhood in Salina, Kansas. Like most teenagers in love, we sought ways to have time to spend alone together talking about…everything.

The block she lived on was especially long because it was a large triangle. I even remember her saying the first time, "Let's go for a walk. This is a long block and we can spend more time together." In my romantic mind, it will always be a special time and so I wrote a poem about it…and her. I called it:

*Just one more walk...one more time to take her*
*hand to hold in mine.*
*One more walk 'round the block to see if there's*
*any chance that she'd love me.*
*I love her so much...that's for sure...this pretty*
*Kansas girl with a heart so pure*

*I hope one day she will say, "Yes" to the*
*proposal I make that day.*
*But for now I'm content to meet...where she*
*lives on Harold Street*

*Our eyes first met on a beautiful fall day in a*
*Salina, Kansas Woolworth store.*
*I came in not knowing the direction I was going*
*or who was on the other side of that door.*

*I sat at the lunch counter amidst all the
noise...and there she was with such beauty and
poise.
That for me to reveal how attracted I was...was
just not the kind of thing a young man does.*

*I ordered coffee and we struck up a chat and I
felt so comfortable that in a moment flat...
I drank the coffee and we continued our chat.*

*I tried not to stare...said goodbye and walked
away...But I knew my life was about to change
that day.*

*I left the store, to the corner I headed and tried
to put it out of my mind...
But try as I might, she was still such a sight, this
girl so beautiful and kind.*

*I stopped in my tracks, felt I had to turn
back...didn't even make it halfway.*

*My head was awhirl over this beautiful girl and
in my heart there began to burn a desire to
change my course and return.
I walked back in the store and decided to order
more coffee from the girl with that smile. I
feared she'd think it odd that I was back so
soon... since I hadn't been gone for a while...*

*But we began sharing as God began pairing two
souls to come together...
For who knows how a miracle grows...a
miracle that would last forever.*

*So protective was I that I planned, do or die,
how to get to her house each day.
By any measure you protect what you treasure.
As an airman with no car I'd hitch a ride to her
house not far and make them drop me off ten
blocks away.*

*I'd walk down the street with her address kept
discrete and looked forward to spending the
day.
And now these years later, our love has grown
greater from a meeting in a Woolworth store.*

*There's no one to compare to the girl with raven
hair and those blue eyes that sparkle so clear.
I prayed she'd be mine, that our hearts would
entwine...and we'd share a love so dear.*

*And it all began in a Woolworth store with a
miracle from God above...*

*And the blessings of a place called Harold
Street and those walks with the girl I love.*

Chapter 2


*Fiddlesticks*


This next poem is actually the last one I wrote shortly before Janna's passing. It's funny how ideas come to you. There was no rhyme (no pun intended) or reason for why I came up with the name Fiddlesticks.

I think I may have been watching the old western TV show *Gunsmoke* and one of the characters, a barefoot hillbilly girl, actually shouted *"Fiddlesticks!"* It's a term not used much anymore that meant disagreement, such as "Oh, fiddlesticks."

When I heard the word, I remembered a child's game I played when I was a boy called "Pick Up Sticks." It was basically a game of physical and mental skill involving a bunch of multi-colored sticks that looked like very large, long toothpicks. They would be dumped in a pile and the object of the game is for a player to pick up more sticks than any of the other players without disturbing the other sticks. There are variations of the game but the winner is, of course, the player with the most sticks at the end.

For some reason the name stuck in my head when I heard it and oddly enough the next thought was about a mule, not a game. Well Festus, who was Sheriff Matt Dillon's sidekick on the show, rode a mule. Well, that sort of morphed into what you're about to hear. The story of a mule, or more accurately two mules, one of whom was named:

*Fiddlesticks*

*(Read with sort of a "sashay rhythm")*


*Fiddlesticks was a stubborn mule...dumb as a*
*five foot tree.*
*But Fiddlesticks weren't so dumb as you'd*
*think...on this you might agree.*


*He didn't really cotton to runnin' and a trottin'*
*like most o' them horses there do.*
*Instead he'd sashay, oh just any old way, just*
*fer a bail o' hay or two.*


*One day though came Whinney...that was her*
*name...a little skinny...But a right cute lookin'*
*mule she was too.*


*Fiddlesticks was eatin,' mindin' his business*
*when a fleetin' glance caught his eye.*
*Yep, it was Whinney, a little bit skinny, but she*
*also was kinda shy.*

*She sidled up beside him and said., "Watcha doin' hidin' that hay all alone fer yerself?" He said, "Weren't hidin' none at all…found it there in the stall…weren't keepin' it alone fer myself."*

*She said, "What's yer name anyway. He said, "Fiddlesticks and hey, I didn't catch your name when you came."*

*She said, "Whinney's my name for sure and I just might be the cure for why you're actin' so blue.*

*'Cause if you had a friend, just might be in the end, there's someone out there for you…*

*So why don't we saunter down the road over yonder and see what there is to be seen*

*Could be you could end up a King...and I'd sure like to be Queen."*

*Well, Fiddlesticks and Whinney went up the road together sharin' their path in life... Fiddlesticks and Whinney, just a little skinny...Fiddlesticks had found him a wife.*

Chapter 3


*The Journey*


Spoiler Alert! Don't go to the end. This poem will be much more enjoyable if you just let the end creep up on you. No, it's not a horror story, but it does have a surprise ending.

I wish I could remember the inspiration for this one, but I wrote it in 1996 and the thought process is unfortunately vague anymore. Let's just say, like a stormy sea, it has progressed to the point of churning up a lot of thought. Try to make it through the first line without lisping. That should be clue enough. Here is the story of:

*The Journey*

*Seven swarthy South Seas sailors set sail on a*
*ship one day…*
*their plans were laid out and off with a shout*
*they sailed for a land far away…*

*Not far out to sea one got sick…and while*
*leaning o'er the bow he did slip…lost his footing*
*for sure, he slipped and fell o'er…and…now*
*there were left…only six…*

*Six sailors to guide things the rest of the*
*way…and still try to keep each alive…when*
*suddenly number six…he up and took*
*sick…died…and now there were five.*

*The others considered their plight, as the ship*
*tossed wildly on the waves that night…but not*
*enough care was taken before…and another*
*rolled off…and now there were… four.*

*The waves tossed higher and the four tried
harder to keep their ship on the seas…
but the winds grew stronger, one's grip grew
weaker…he was blown off and now there were
three.*

*When suddenly from out of the East there came
the sound of a gale…and it roared and poured
rain as if out of a boot…and that was followed
by hail.*

*Such a storm they'd not seen, since they left Port
Serene…
and sailed off on the ocean blue…so the three
grabbed a line, but one not in time…and guess
what…now there were two.*

*Two sailors under heaven, when at first there
were seven…to sail o'er the Southern seas…*

*when in the midst of this storm, the sound of
alarm...tells one sailor, "This is no fun."*

*But then there's a slip...he loses his grip...falls
over, and now there is one.*

*When suddenly the ship is tossed...wildly both to
and fro...and the motion of it seems strange,
says he, as if it's something I know.*

*The movement and the shaking were now
becoming real...
and our swarthy little sailor's wond'ring... what
is this I feel?*

*When he suddenly opens his eyes to see a most
comforting and wonderful sight.
It's Mom...saying, "Johnny, you've been
dreaming. Now lay down...go to sleep...and
goodnight."*

Chapter 4


*The Way Home*


Aren't you glad you paid attention to the spoiler alert?  You didn't? Well, there's more. This next poem I also wrote in 1996. It was written much later after I had accepted Jesus as my Lord and Savior. That's a phrase a lot of Christians use to proclaim their faith, but to a world that does not know Him, it leaves open a lot of questions.

When I wrote this poem the Lord inspired me to "tell them about the way home." I thought to myself *what do you mean…the way home*? God said, "Heaven."

When we go on a trip these days we usually use a GPS, but before that, we had a road map. When we're born we came from somewhere …and we're going somewhere. This is *not* our home. This is a journey. From the moment you are born, two things are present. You have a huge empty place in your spirit. It's a definite place and you've begun a journey. We're going somewhere; we're not just an amoeba drifting through the cosmos.

My father was a driven businessman, a car dealer. He didn't like to lose. When he died, my mother told me I just stood there for a long time at his casket and watched him. I suddenly realized *he really was not there.* I mean I recognized the body lying there, but that wasn't the Bob Worden I knew. *He was gone!* He had left!  I don't know where he went, but he was gone!

On Christmas Day 2021 I lost my beloved wife, the one person whom I knew better than anyone on earth and I *knew* she was gone. Her spirit had left.

Janna found the roadmap home on September 22, 1973. I found the roadmap on June 14, 1974.

As you journey through life, you will try to fill that empty space in your soul with a lot of things—sex, drugs, money, career, alcohol, friends (some good; some bad). Lots of stuff. Unfortunately even the wealthiest people in the world have found that none of it lasts. Some, though they have everything they ever wanted, take their own life.

That's because God meant that empty place to be filled with Him. Not that other stuff. He even gave us a road map to bring us:

*The Way Home*

*We're born into this life like ships upon the
sea...our destinies a mystery...no way for us to
see.*

*That's why God gives His word to us...with love
and with perfection...that we would know the
way through it...and find the right direction.*

*His Word is powerful and wholesome, perfect in
every way...each sentence crafted fully to help
us all each day.*

*That over our life's journey we'd know which
way to turn...which life to touch, and just how
much... we ourselves would learn.*

*It's called the Holy Bible but it has another
name...the Word of God is one we know but
that's not quite the same..*

*The other name you see is a common one for
sure; in fact, so simple is it...yet perfect to the
core.*

*Like ships alone we're set upon the sea of life to
deal with all our struggles...in a world of sin
and strife.*

*But now as God would have it there has always
been a way...it's the promise of His Word...and
the things to us He'd say...*

*To make this trip we need no map...nor
compass...nor a sextant...we only need to hear
God's voice... and thereby be expectant.*

*For the Holy Bible is God's roadmap to the
world. His promises, His blessings...and His
judgments all unfurled.*

*The Bible therefore has another name alone. It's God's roadmap for our life...and it points to..."The Way Home."*

Chapter 5


*Short Work*


This is a poem you can read between the kitchen and the living room unless you live in a mansion.

The shortest verse in the Bible is John 11:35 "Jesus wept."

Well, I can't top that, but I came close in 1988 when I wrote the shortest poem I've ever written. For all you grammatical genius's out there, I nicknamed it a "Terse Verse."

It will also make this the shortest chapter in the book.

In fact this intro is longer than the poem is. Here is:

*I sat and sat and wondered that…*

*this poem would be so small.*

*but then again, I thought again,*

*it's just a poem...that's all!*

Every time I read this to someone I get the urge to cap it off at the end with that Bugs Bunny thing…" Nyaaa…what's up Doc?"

Okay, onward and upward.

Chapter 6

*An Abundance of Rain*

There is a time coming in the world of changes we've never yet seen. In fact ancient scripture foretold, even as Christ hung on a cross on Calvary, that times and seasons would mark great fulfilled prophesies.

Well, fact is, every prophesy concerning Jesus' coming to earth was fulfilled; the only one left is His returning. And that will happen as well. There are people out there with all manner of charts and things who claim they known when. Anything that counters the Bible is considered heresy and that's heresy.

In Acts 1:7 it says, "It is not for you to know times or seasons that the Father has fixed by his own authority." So, short answer; Nobody knows.

In 1988 The United States launches Operation Praying Mantis against Iranian naval forces in the largest naval battle since World War II.

During the Israeli–Palestinian conflict: An independent State of Palestine is proclaimed by the Palestinian National Council.

It was during this time I was inspired to write a poem called:

*There is, in these times, the ominous sound of a*
*sound that's not yet heard…*
*the warnings which come down through the*
*ages in the pages of God's Word.*

*It's the sound, said Elijah, of an abundance of*
*rain, for the prophets did foretell…*
*of the coming of the Prince of Peace and the*
*defeat of death & hell.*

*On Calvary's dark hill that day, the sky was*
*black with clouds*
*and as he hung on a cross so still, Jesus shouted*
*aloud…*

*"Forgive them, Father, forgive them for they*
*know not what they do"*
*The words ring down through the ages. They*
*were meant for me and you.*

*Elijah made an ancient promise of a powerful
abundance of rain...
and in God's infinite plan for man, the rain...will
come again.*

*Make your house ready, my friend, make sure
it's on the rock...
and of yourself and your family, be sure you
take full stock.*

*What sorts of things do you allow to come into
your door?
What kinds of things do your eyes perceive as
you wander through a store?*

*Keep watch for your soul, my friend...keep
watch both night and day.
Don't take God for granted and don't forget to
pray.*

*For as Elijah so long ago, through the power of*

*God, brought rain,*

*He will once again, through the power of God,*

*bring an abundance of rain…again.*

## Chapter 7

*Snow*

The year was 1980 and I was working the evening shift at the television station. (sounds like an intro to *Dragnet*, doesn't it) Anyway, that particular night, we were in the midst of a dandy...and I mean a *dandy* snowstorm. Most blizzards outside the television studio on Smith Hill in Deerfield, New York, were noteworthy.

It was a slow news night, nothing much to cover except perhaps an occasional accident among those brave enough to go out and drive in that stuff.

I had some time, so I decided, "You know what? I'll write a poem about the storm and have our guys shoot some footage to go with it. If nothing else, it'll give me another story to fill an otherwise lackluster block of news."

Sorry, I can't show you the footage but, well, you've seen snowstorms. The script was called:

*Snow*

*Last night as I pondered the clear, cold skies,*
*I couldn't believe what was before my eyes.*


*Another forecast of snow, they said…the one*
*thing, right now, that most of us dread.*
*But giving little thought to the consequence, I*
*pulled another blanket over my head.*


*When dawn arrived, just as promised, there it*
*was, like the springtime return of Santa Claus…*


*Snow! Snow! Not a little, but a lot, covering*
*everything in April, leaving empty nary a spot.*
*They say it'll be nice Easter day but as the*
*snowflakes continued to fall our way.*


*I couldn't help wonder if our wintry plight might*
*better prompt us to catch a flight*

*to a more temperate zone or at least we might
dream we've flown to a warmer place*

*where cold fronts and lows will stop dealing
those devastating blows.*

*How nice it would be to water the lawn or head
North and do a little lazy fishin'.
Now is that so wrong?*

*We sit and watch the snowflakes swirl and
wonder why this crazy whirl of springtime
weather gets us down.*

*Then the answer comes with ease when we hear
the little tease of better weather on Easter day.*

*But for now, it's hard to take...this business of
winter wind and flake and we wonder if the sun
is really there!*

*Give us a good one Mr. Weatherman, something we can share. For Easter day, sunny skies...no snow, moderate and fair.*

*Well, at any rate, those are my views...I'm Bill Worden for Newschannel-2 News.*

Chapter 8


*Red Ryder Spurs*


I wrote this poem in 1996 during an especially nostalgic period when I was going through some old photographs of our family when I was a boy. If you read my book, *A Kansas Love Story*, you may remember I lived for a time in South Bend, Indiana. My folks lived on a farm. We actually just rented the house.

Back in the early fifties there was a popular cowboy TV show based on the comic book cowboy character Red Ryder. It was sponsored by a well-known shredded wheat cereal company and they were offering a free pair of cowboy spurs for any "Buckaroo" who could save up the appropriate number of cardboard biscuit separators in every box. Each box had two.

I don't remember the required number, but I saved them all up and my mother sent them in for me. I was never so excited when the spurs arrived, though after a week or so of me "jingling" around the house, Mom suggested I wear them outside where good cowboys play.

Anyway it was during that flood of memories I was inspired to write:

*Red Ryder Spurs*


*Back in the fifties when the desperados rode,*

*there once lived a lad on a quiet country road...*


*He lived for Saturdays and Red Ryder*

*spurs...and the good guys beat the bad guys...*

*'cause the good guys wore the spurs.*


*The bad guys wore spurs too but they never*

*made no noise but the good guys spurs would*

*jingle, just like good ol' Roy's...*

*Now Billy'd watch Red Ryder, put his spurs on*

*too...*

*and eat his shredded wheat...then wrestle a*

*Buckaroo.*


*Good Ol' shredded wheat it was that started*

*Billy's day...*

*wheat in the morning then Red Ryder then on*

*out to play.*

*Livin' on a farm had its own kinda charm and
pretendin' to be Red Ryder was part of it...
but those spurs...those jingle-jangle spurs...they
were what made little Billy love it.*

*And now was his chance to have at a glance, his
own pair of Red Ryder spurs...
'cause the company, you see, was offerin' 'em
free...fer just sev'ral box tops and they're yers...*

*Well, he finally saved 'em all, packed 'em
up...said, "Mom, don't stall...these gotta get out
to the place with the shredded wheat.*

*They're the ones with the falls on the box...with
the water goin' over the rocks..they're the only
kind Red Ryder'd ever eat."*

*So with that she did hasten, for she saw li'l bill
was wastin'...no time practicin' his jingle-jangle
walk...*

*Every Saturday for Bill was shredded wheat
and... well...learnin' to talk the Red Ryder kind-
a talk..*

*But it wouldn't be long before Billy'd hear a
knock at the door...and the sound of the
mailman saying, "Hey Billy...ya' got a package
here, but it jingles in my ear...and frankly, it
sounds kinda silly."*

*Well, he tore at that box wrapped tightly, and
then suddenly beamed a smile brightly...
when he opened it and saw what was inside.*

*They jingled and they jangled and they weren't a
bit mangled...
his Red Ryder spurs...they'd arrived.*

*So the moral of this story...well, there really
weren't none...or we might have changed the
ending just a bit.*

*For the thoughts of Bill were ponderin'...just where he'd be a wanderin' but no problem...now he got his kit.*

*So let's just say Bill's treat was in a box o' shredded wheat...and it didn't take no money for which to wrangle.*

*No sir-mam this was free...from the cowboy on TV. Some Red Ryder spurs...that jingle-jangle.*

Chapter 9

*The Alligator*

When I was in the Air Force, we were taught the importance of obeying commands on the battlefield. In short, disobedience to commands could cost your life and those of your comrades in arms.

One of the first words a child learns is the word "No!" That rebellious spirit we're born with emerges early and in short, they like to challenge your authority, not realizing you're only trying to keep them from doing something that may hurt them.

Back in 1988, I was watching a documentary on alligator hunters and just suddenly got this idea to write a tale (again, no pun intended) about an alligator and a little girl.

I decided to turn it into a story with a moral about the importance of obedience, specifically the little girl and the consequences of her *dis*-obedience to her parents warning.

In my fictional tale (again, no pun…well, never mind) the little girl decides to disobey her parents who tell her to stay away from the pond because of:

*The Alligator*

*T'was in a briny swamp one day a little lass had
gone to play and told her Mom and Dad she'd
be home later.*

*She knew they didn't want her to take the time to
wander...to the swampy place 'cause of the
alligator.*

*Quite contrary to their teaching, she counted it
"so much preachin." and choosing to ignore her
Mom and Dad.*

*Little Mary found no fun in minding and didn't
think she'd be finding the briney swamp would
be all that bad.*

*She took along some food to help her sustain
her "mood" and she chose to go the one place
that she shouldn't.*

*Her mother told her long ago that down there
where dark waters flow, swim animals whose
company to enjoy, she wouldn't.*

*Well, off she went to the briny pond, so secretly
did she abscond that both Mom and Dad were
rightfully offended.*

*But one thing is for sure her attitude needed a
cure, and this may not have been what was
intended.*

*Mary reached the briny swamp that day and
promptly sat down to play and began to look for
some good, good, goody to eat.*

*Well, the water began to tipple, and she thought
she heard a ripple and turned around to see
what was the ruckus.*

*Just as she did, her foot suddenly slid and she had slipped a little further into the muckus.*

*The next thing that she saw was not a pleasant sight—a slinky, slimy, slithery thing that swims by day and night.*

*Little did she think she'd be hurt or even that she'd done wrong, but if it's up to this alligator, she won't be here for long.*

*The moral of this story's a simple one you see, for obedience to rules is basic for you and me. Mary could not accept the blame for the very things she did. She'd cast the blame on other things, the fault on her to rid.*

*And so the 'gators tummy, being rather large and hungry started searching for what to fill this massive crater.*

*He took one look at Miss Marple said, "She'd outdo any carple," and so the story ends.*

*The 'gator....ate her!*

Chapter 10

*The Saturday Mechanic*

This poem, written in 1988, was one of the first I had written and I drew from personal experience.

What father out there has not looked forward to the weekend and perhaps a project or two to work on, be it a repair on the house or working on that beloved hot rod in the garage?

Everything is laid out according to plan when he suddenly realizes there are others in the family who have needs as well.

Well, I don't think there's much more to describe what happens to:

*The Saturday Mechanic*

*There he is 'fore the sun comes up, prowlin'*
*through his box of tools...gathering prods and*
*pliers and such and his real good craftsman*
*rule.*

*Pay no mind this well-intended fella has no idea*
*what he's doing...the idea here is to save a buck*
*and get the old crate going.*

*Well, let's see, the day lies ahead and nary a*
*care has he. He's all alone and not to be*
*bothered, he and his two-eighty-three.*

*First things first, the coffee's hot and the donuts*
*just arrived but his wife just informed him they*
*have to be somewhere at five.*

*Well, that didn't help his attitude much 'cause he*
*thought he had all day...to size up his problems*

*with the two-eighty-three and then later hit the
hay.*

*So quickly he gathered his tools and his stool
and his manual and his creeper and crawled
under the two-eighty-three to find what part was
the leaker.*

*Just then, little Sara ran into the garage and
said, "Whatcha' doin' Dad? Can you come out
here and fix my bike; it really looks kinda bad."*

*So off he went out front to take care of the
problem at hand.*
*Turns out the problem was minor; the bike just
fell off its stand.*

*On his way back to the car, son Johnny said,
"Dad, got a minute.?*

*I can't figure out where this thing goes, and why
it won't fit in it."*

*"Sure, no problem", said Dad, "it's one of these
thing-a-ma-bobs...It fits right here like the two-
eighty-three. There that'll do the job."*

*So on to the garage he went when his wife
hollered, "Honey, please come
quick...Something on the dishwasher's stuck and
I can't get it to unstuck."*

*Well that job turned out to be a three-hour one
at that. By the time he was done, the clock said
three o'clock flat.*

*Only two hours left to the whole day...the day
he thought that he had.
So he crawled back under the two-eighty-three
and found the part that went bad.*

*Fact is not a thing he could do, this part was*

*totally shot...The motor was fine, the*

*transmission too but this part had gone to pot.*


*Now the moral of this tale should be easily*

*comprehended that a Saturday mechanic can be*

*easily upended...and there's no need for the*

*family to panic...*


*For these are just the ways, you see, of the*

*Saturday mechanic.*

Chapter 11

*This Time for Eternity*

My beloved wife, Janna, passed on Christmas day 2021 and with that, I find myself suddenly thrust into a new world without her. Even those words "without her" sound strange; hurtful if you will.

Only those who have lost a loved spouse can relate to this feeling—just me in a big house full of stuff. Things collected through a lifetime together. Some things brought by each of us into the marriage from our childhood years before we even knew each other.

Heirlooms of times and ancestral past fill the shelves and nooks and crannies and yet, the only treasures that matter to me now are pictures of her. Some counselors will tell you to take them down; put them away. That's not going to happen. Her pictures are sort of a comfort to me, a comfortable connection to her.

I can't avoid them; they're right there in front of me and I love it because it's almost like she's still here. Do I talk to her? You bet I do. I always did. I always will and even more so when I run to her arms in eternity.

Jesus brought us together and I can't wait until the day that he brings us together again forever.

It's upon these thoughts that I base the final chronological poem I wrote in what may be my final book since I have no inspiration to write another. And how right and fitting it is that it's a poem about…her.

*This Time for Eternity*

*I wish I could forever live in the fifty-nine years*
*you were with me.*
*But I know that forever will go on and our joy*
*will ever be.*

*Simple times of just sitting together,*
*didn't matter what kind of weather.*

*Our days were sunny and bright*
*because your presence made me take flight.*

*My life didn't start on my birthday you know…It*
*really began with you.*
*And God knew well what we'd be planning and*
*what we're about to do.*

*It's very hard now knowing you're gone.*
*The nights are cold and the days are long.*

*My heart, my soul, my best friend you were.*

*Just seeing you in the morning gave me a stir.*


*Where does the time go? Where have the years gone?*

*I guess I sit and ponder too much. But is that all so wrong?*

*I can't just take those years and throw them all away.*

*I have no choice but to think of you ...each and every day.*


*And somehow it makes it easier to concentrate on you*

*than to relegate our memories to a box of pictures or two.*


*You'll never really be gone to me; not now, not tomorrow; not ever.*

*Because our hearts and souls are so entwined that we're destined to be together.*

*And so it will happen one day when God decides
to call me home,
when upon this fertile bristly patch I will no
longer roam*

*But instead will find myself transformed again
to a place of unimagined wonder.*

*Where frightening things no longer manifest
in sounds of light and thunder*

*but rather God brings us to a place of peace and
rest
when I come to realize He had for me the very
best.*

*Just as the day I met you, and knowing there
could be no other
who would bring me joy and happiness I could
never find in another.*

*God brought you to me years ago to unite our hearts you see*

*and now He's finally done it again… only this time… for eternity.*

Chapter 12


*Thirty Years and Three*


Back in 1988, I was into a real writing spurt. (Funny I never wrote a book). Anyway I did begin writing poems, several of them. Some were of a religious nature, some personal, some humorous, some serious.

One day I was thinking of how short a life Jesus had—thirty-three years. That's it! Thirty-three years on this earth, and yet there is not a single human being on the face of the earth who has impacted mankind as much as He. Why? Well, I believe He really is the Son of God.

Who else could do the things He did and affect the world the way He did *for centuries.* So, I began jotting a few lines about His short life and called it:

Thirty Years and Three

*Thirty years and three...the years He gave to
me.*
*The depth and length and breadth to some... are
difficult to see.*

*For how a single carpenter could so severely
change it...*
*a world so steeped in sin and hate and thereby
rearrange it.*

*His presence was so simple...so nondescript,
and yet,*
*His life would shape man's destiny...His blood
would be to let.*

*For the spirit of man loved himself so much, he
could not love God too.*
*And therefore put God out of sight... deceiving
me and you.*

72

*The carpenter whose hands were rough whose
heart would surely flood...
with love to flow for every person...with every
drop of blood.*

*The Word itself would he ordain to spread
among the world...through his Father he would
come...and so the Word unfurled.*

*Brought to sick and dying men, his miracles
would state,
that God the Father, by his power, would
overcome sin and hate.*

*Thirty and three years for me...to you He'd give
them too.
And in that space of time He'd change the
course of history through.*

*That march up Calvary he would take...his trial
nearly ended.*

*For loving man, he'd suffer so... the heathen, he offended.*

*They said he was a criminal but he was gentle as a dove*
*and the only crime he committed... was that he offered merely love.*

*The nails were driven deeper still...each one for you and me, for by our sin He suffered so...that day upon the tree.*

*Thirty years and three were gone...His time for you, for me.*
*But by his power and by His might, they'd set the captive free.*

*Neither any noble thing you do...nor I will ever pay,*
*for what took place at that dark hour....on Golgotha's hill that day.*

*And so it was for this carpenter...the Lamb, the chosen one*

*who looked unto His Father and said, "Father, it is done!"*


*But the story doesn't end here...for Satan was offended*

*and little did he know...his plan would be amended.*


*The Father of all glory, you see would bring him to his knees*

*and Jesus, in His power...demanded all the keys.*


*He opened every prison gate... of Satan's foul horde*

*and set the sinner free to worship... Jesus Christ, the lord.*


*No historic date in time.... could mean so much to me,*

*as those few precious years of life...His...thirty years...and three!*

Chapter 13

*What Archie Did*

In 1996, I wrote a poem inspired by my own childhood. When I was a boy, we played with cap pistols. We'd load a roll of red gunpowder dots into our "six gun" and play we were cowboys.

Those were innocent days when the thought of shooting someone was make believe and only the "bad guys" died anyway.

I concocted this story out of that—only the weapon wasn't a cap pistol. It was a totally made up toy I named a "Gumball Rocket."

There I go creating layers of fiction again. I took two words, *gumball,* which was usually a big candy-coated ball of bubble gum and the word *rocket.* Well, you know what that is.

Anyway in the story, this was a toy a boy might carry in his pocket and throw on the ground and it would go *bang*! (They actually did have something like that but that's not what it was called.)

I needed to create something for *my* world that would fit the poem. I guess you can file that under poetic license.

Hence we find out:

*What Archie Did*


*The tale's been oft told what Archie did that day.*
*He lived to tell his loved ones of the fame that*
*came his way.*


*How stepping out of his safe warm home would*
*cost him plenty too…*
*and leave a story for generations for the likes of*
*me and you.*


*Not much, you'd expect from a kid not taller*
*than a spicket on the side of a house.*
*But with Archie, there was a lot more, you*
*see…than a shy little, tiny little mouse.*


*Archie's favorite thing was bringin' the bad guys*
*in and twice a week or so he'd do just that.*
*Now Archie was eight, you see…the oldest boy*
*of three…and he was about to leave the bad*
*guys flat.*

*Believe it or not he etched out a place for*
*himself in history one day*
*when he foiled a holdup, arrested the bad guys,*
*and still had time to play.*

*He had his allowance in his overalls pocket,*
*planned to buy some candy and a five-cent*
*Gumball Rocket.*

*When out of nowhere came two men...gangsters*
*of ill repute*
*who demanded money from the cashier, or else*
*they said...they'd shoot.*

*Little Archie stayed outa sight, hidden down*
*behind the counter.*
*The cashier said, "There's no money" but the*
*bad guys had reason to doubt her.*

*They reached in the drawer and pulled out much*
*more money than they'd seen in a while*

*when suddenly from behind Archie jumped up
and blind-sided both of them with a smile...*

*Oh, there was something more that we didn't tell
you; before those bad guys were scared by a
bang!*

*They quickly started shakin' not knowin' he was
fakin'; they just stood there and listened to his
harangue.*

*They thought it was a gun, but it was really only
one of little Archie's Gumball Rockets.
He'd eaten 'em all, except for one ball that he
had left inside his shirt pocket.*

*Well, the story's short and sweet and for Archie
what a treat
to see those bad guys put their hands up and
stop.*

*They thought they'd been had and the cashier
was glad and the first thing she did was a call a
cop.*

*So there you have it straight how a little boy of
eight put the bad guys on the police docket.
Little Archie did it beautifully...did his duty
dutifully...and he did it...with a five-cent
Gumball Rocket.*

Chapter 14

*My Wife*

1988 was, it seems, my most productive year when it came to writing poems. I don't know if it was inspiration or just a lot of free time, but nonetheless, I wrote a lot of them.

This next one was fairly short and, yes, it was about Janna. If you knew her, you would know she didn't like a lot of attention. She even asked why I had written so many poems about her. My answer was clever. I said, "Well, you're good subject matter." So, I called it:

*My Wife*

*I still can now remember her, in wisps of
younger days
when the scent of Hemlock and pleasant things
would remind me of her ways.
When caught so short by Janna, I could scarcely
turn away
and how slowly time would pass for me to see
her one more day.*

*Hair so black and skin so white and a smile that
brought such blessing…
and a gingham dress of lavender that sees me
now confessing.*

*That since a small boy I saw her face…the face
of the one I would love…
with a sweetness to mother our children and the
gentleness of her love.*

*For God so loved me, He gave me a girl to*
*brighten all of my days...*
*who gives all her love and cares and always*
*offers praise.*

*So now I see my wife, oh Lord, in ways not*
*known before...*
*when through young eyes, still blind with youth*
*I had not gone through that door.*

*But now the joy of living for God reveals itself*
*so clear...*
*that now I see my lover's eyes. They're Janna's*
*eyes so dear.*

Chapter 15

*The Bible & the TV Guide*

I have no idea when I wrote this because I forgot to put a date on it, but I've had it for many years. It was inspired by a memory of my home growing up. There was always a Bible and a TV Guide nearby, though I don't know that anyone ever read it much—the Bible that is.

As for the TV Guide? Why that thing got picked up everyday without fail. Well, how else would we know what was going to happen if we didn't pick up the TV guide to find out? See where I'm going here? No further explanation needed. It's simply:

*The Bible & the TV Guide*

*They lay there on the table, side by side…*

*the Holy Bible and the TV Guide.*

*One is well-worn, but cherished with pride.*
*oh, not the Holy Bible. We're talkin' bout the*
*TV Guide.*

*One is used daily to help folks decide.*
*No, not the Bible…it's the good ol' TV Guide.*

*As the pages are turned, what shall they see?*
*Oh, what does it matter? Turn on the TV.*

*Then confusion reigns, they can't all agree…*
*what shall they watch on the old TV?*

*So they open the book in which they confide…*
*no, it's not the Bible…it's the old TV Guide.*


*The Word of God is seldom read.*
*Oh maybe a verse or two before they go to bed.*


*Exhausted and sleepy, as tired as can be…*
*not from reading the Bible. No, from watching*
*TV.*


*So back to the table, side by side*
*lays the Holy Bible and the old TV Guide.*


*No time for prayer, no time for the Word,*
*the plan of salvation seldom heard.*


*Forgiveness of sin so sure and so free…*
*is found in the Bible, John 3:16…not on TV.*

Chapter 16

91

*A Moment in the Tomb*

Another jewel from 1988 turned out to be, I feel, one of my better efforts. I was in my office one day reading about a visit to Israel and visiting the tomb of Jesus. I wondered what it would be like to actually stand there in that tomb and realize the historic and cataclysmic event that happened there. That's when I was inspired to write:

*A Moment in the Tomb*

*A moment calm and quiet, like nothing ever
known...broke forth upon my spirit as I stood
there all alone.*

*And I began to realize just what occurred that
day as Jesus hung there on the cross and my
sins were washed away.*

*The sky with eerie blackness, as if to say, "It's
true," proclaimed with rolls of thunder, "He
died for me and you."*

*The tomb awaits and soon to come a battle
twixt heav'n and hell.
For three days inside these walls, only Jesus the
story could tell.*

*He would descend to the depths of the earth
alone and meet the adversary.*

*For the devil and his hordes had won. They
were dancing and making merry.*

*The Son of God is gone at last; they thought
their work was finished...
But even as Jesus hung on the cross, their power
was diminished.*

*He arrived in power and might that day and
proclaimed, "I'll take the keys...You won't do
this again, Satan...now get down on your
knees."*

*While in the depths of the earth alone, Jesus
began taking
the prisoners of sin whom Satan had told, their
lives had been forsaken.*

*And suddenly, in that same moment, I was
transported to the tomb...*

*And beheld the wondrous Son of God whose
presence filled the room.*

*He told me not to worry, my heavenly home is
secure...that the promises He made me are
eternally guaranteed and sure.*
*And as I saw him leave, there was no hint of
gloom...*
*For he showed me his wondrous promise...in
that moment in the tomb.*

Chapter 17

*The Road Map*

This poem, also written in 1988, may put you in mind of an earlier one in the book called "The Way Home."

What's it like to wake up when you've never been asleep? Well, that's what it's like when you're born. We're already alive and awake and we're about to begin a journey that will take some of us many years to complete—a journey through life's loves, joys, pitfalls, failures and victories.

Without a road map for life, though, we're already in big trouble. The Bible is:

*The Road Map*

*I've lived a life more half than not...and never*
*contemplated much*
*for I've few memories as a tot and as I grew,*
*never dated much.*
*But this I tell you true this day the things you're*
*about to hear,*
*reflect an older, wiser man...whose time is*
*drawing near.*


*To understand the things of life... a few years*
*can't attain.*
*for though our problems may come quick...the*
*answers come in vain.*


*We take our thoughts in youth and view them*
*through young eyes,*
*but God's plan can only work as long as we are*
*wise.*

*How foolish we can be too, in youth, never think
or try
to talk with the great God who made us but
merely sit and sigh.*

*And often wonder why we're here... and what
our purpose is...
and try and picture God as authoring some sort
of cosmic quiz.*

*With age comes living, the hurts, the wages, the
loves, and all the pain,
but through it all, we finally come...around full
circle again.*

*For the secret of eternity rests in knowing the
God of light
the One whose presence is **always** there...in the
day and through the night.*

*To realize this life-long sojourn is intended for a*
*higher goal...*
*to reach the end with blessings...and your name*
*on Heaven's roll.*

*When suddenly life's journey turns a corner and*
*heads another way*
*to a bright and brand new morning...to a grand*
*and brand new day.*

*And so it goes, this infinite plan that God has*
*made for all of man...*
*and now the choice is yours to make...a life*
*eternal...yours to take.*

*Make your choice, and make it well...for eternity*
*is long in hell.*

*The things of life will draw you now,*
*but in life's shadows, they'll furrow your brow.*

*Choose you this day whom you will serve, and*
*think of the things that you'll deserve.*
*Redeem the time, for it is nigh... God's word is*
*written upon the sky.*

*That the prophets would testify...to that which*
*has been said,*
*that the sun would soon turn dark and the moon*
*would soon turn red.*

*It is all true, you see, the words of this book are*
*true,*
*so listen well my people...for these words are*
*written for you.*

*The things which were said and done of old,*
*which still stand to this day,*
*are things which testify of Jesus...of His life and*
*of His way.*

*When we're born into this world, on a journey
we must go.
and o'er life's waves we'll move as we're tossed
both to and fro.*

*But one thing is for certain...as across this sea
we roam.
The Father has given us a road map...to bring
us fully home.*

Chapter 18


*The Thin Red Line*


This is a somewhat later writing put together in 2000. There is a crucifixion scene in the 1953 film *The Robe* in which the centurion, played by actor Richard Burton, who crucified Jesus, is standing at the foot of the cross.

A storm is picking up and he leans forward, places his hand on the cross and suddenly he feels something warm trickling down his hand. It is a small stream of blood from Jesus.

Frightened, the centurion jerks his hand away and the camera follows the trail of blood as it falls to the ground, mixes with a stream of water from the falling rain and makes its way down the hill.

That scene inspired me to write:

*The Thin Red Line*


*The red line, so thin and rare. It's place was*

*odd, it didn't belong there.*

*It trailed from town to a place on a hill; its trail*

*a message for the world to be still...*


*It took some time for my eyes to behold. Its*

*power and strength for years to unfold...*

*A message of love and peace to portray...the*

*power of this line exists to this day.*


*Neither name nor place nor power can be as*

*important as that line of love is to me.*

*It speaks through the ages the language of*

*love...a message from God's Son and His*

*Father above...*

*So now as I traverse the way of the cross I find*

*myself with words at a loss...*

*to describe to others what this line means to*

*me...to live life in joy and of sin to be free.*


*For the line was his blood poured out for us*

*all...the thin red line to that hill oh so tall...*

*His blood shed in full over passing of time...as I*

*look at Dolorosa ...and the thin red line.*

Chapter 19


*Raptured*


At the beginning of this book, I shared that some poems would have surprise endings. This is another one, so fair warning; this is a spoiler alert.

Among the poems I wrote in 1988 was this one. My wife used to say of herself, "When I accepted the Lord as my Savior, I decided to believe all of the Bible or none of it. No gray areas."

In 1st Thessalonians 4:17, Paul is talking about Jesus coming back to earth. And He said, *"Then we who are alive, who are left, will be caught up together with them in the clouds to meet the Lord in the air, and so we will always be with the Lord."*

To every Christian, that's the real deal. It's not a fairy tale. It will happen. Why do we know that? Because virtually every prophecy in the Bible has already come true exactly as it said, from the birth of Jesus to His miraculous resurrection from the tomb.

His disciples went to their horrid deaths willingly because they knew all of it was true. No one willingly dies for something they know to be a lie. According to ancient prophecy, Jesus' return is imminent.

I don't know when it will happen, but it will happen and by all the earthly events of the last one hundred or so years, it appears it's not far off.

That's why I wrote:

*Raptured*

*I spent the better part of my life, and most of my waking hours,*
*contemplating most normal things—birds and bees and flowers.*
*And like most folks who walk this earth, I never gave much of a thought*
*to seeking time alone with God, or trying to be taught...*

*that God loved man enough, to send His only Son...*
*to straighten out this mess down here and ruin Satan's fun.*

*But now you know there's one more thing with which man has to deal...*
*something men will scoff at... and claim is not real.*

*But God's Word so long ago said this would*
*happen too...*
*so consider it as the Bible shows, as just another*
*clue.*

*The rapture of the saints of God will be when*
*the heavens are shaken...*
*and Jesus comes back in glory and then we'll*
*soon be taken.*

*People seem to live their lives as though they*
*were a fable...*
*and like a game of cards their lives are laid*
*upon the table.*

*And one by one, they take their chances, though*
*warned enough by others...*
*that sure as sin, judgment comes... on those who*
*want their "druthers."*

*For as the things God has proclaimed, unfold in
all their fury...
the Son of man will come again... in a cloud
with pow'r and glory.*

*Thus the scriptures have spoken, for God's
Word does not lie...
for when these things will come to pass...your
redemption draweth nigh.*

*I've seen men try to predict his coming through
charts and human reason...
but Jesus said we cannot know the exact time or
the season.*

*Rest assured the time will come when men's
hearts will be taken....
and there will be signs in the sun and the
heavens will be shaken.*

*Take heed that you're deceived, for many will
say "I'm the Lord,"
but what they show to the world will be seen at
the tip of a sword.*

*Earthquakes will happen and sickness and
plagues and famine will everywhere be...
and fearful sights and great signs from heaven,
will be there for all to see.*

*But I say to you this day, this generation will not
pass away...
'til My words are instilled, and My sayings
fulfilled...*

*For now as the time draws near, and millions of
hearts are captured...
those in the Lamb's Book of Life...will all very
soon be rap...!*

Chapter 20

*The 23<sup>rd</sup> Psalm*

I felt this a fitting way to end this book. There are few in the world who don't know or haven't heard the 23<sup>rd</sup> Psalm. It is often repeated in funeral ceremonies because its words so fittingly describe our final relationship to God

I wrote this in 1995 at a time when I was examining my own heart and coming to the realization of my own mortality. I had the blessings of a beautiful wife, a good job, home and family.

But in 1995, having lived more than half my life (and now my future is even smaller), I found the words of the 23<sup>rd</sup> Psalm particularly poignant. I have no fear of death; it's a natural part of being born. I know, without a doubt, where I will be and frankly I can't wait to see

Janna again, for the Bible says, "We will be known as we are known."

And that is why I wrote the poem:

## *The 23rd Psalm*

*The light that God shines on a dark and plaited
world...*
*makes worthy all life created and all creation
unfurled.*


*And if for just one moment, I could touch His
glorious face...*
*I would understand, as David's Psalm, His spirit
to embrace.*


*Shine on...shine on, bright spirit, long after my
days are done...*
*long after my spirit has left and flown unto the
Son...*


*Shine on...shine on, my Lord...let Your spirit
soar in me...*
*give me wisdom and courage and grace to be
part of the bride You see.*

*Let not Your spirit fade, my Lord...nor my sight
before Your eyes...
that I may see the end reward...my
mansion...and my prize.*

*For though I'd be happy as a gatekeeper in the
halls of where You live...
I could never earn Your mercy for the sins that
You forgive...*

*So with Your Psalm before me...I move to turn
back never...
that I may be privileged to dwell...in the house
of the Lord forever.*